TAKING PART IN THE SECOND WORLD WAR

In the Air

Ann Kramer

FRANKLIN WATTS
LONDON • SYDNEY

IN ASSOCIATION WITH

IMPERIAL WAR

MUSEUM

This edition 2011

First published in 2009 by Franklin Watts

Franklin Watts
338 Euston Road
London NW1 3BH

Franklin Watts Australia
Level 17/207 Kent Street
Sydney, NSW 2000

A CIP catalogue record for this book is available
from the British Library

Dewey number: 940.5'44'0922

ISBN: 978 1 4451 0641 0

Printed in China

Franklin Watts is a division of Hachette Children's Books,
an Hachette UK company.

www.hachette.co.uk

Editor: Sarah Ridley
Design: Billin Design Solutions
Editor in Chief: John C. Miles
Art director: Jonathan Hair
Maps: Jason Billin

With many thanks to Nick Hewitt and the staff at the Imperial
War Museum's Document, Sound and Photograph Archives.

Picture credits: All images copyright © Imperial War Museum unless otherwise stated.

Front cover: Front cover: main TR 001442, top right A 042601, bottom right TR 000979, b/g H 004219
Back cover: Top right © Audrey Hale, middle right CH 018005, left CH 011926, b/g H 004219
Insides: Title page CH 001367, p4 CH000740, p5 C 0001785, p6 CH 001373, p7t CH 012263,
p7b CH 001299, p8 CH 001355, p9t HU 049253, P9b CH001829, p10 HU 0731139 © Eastbourne
Gazette, p11 C001512, p12 CH 001367, p13 D 008976, p14t HU 053753, p14b D006847,
p15 CH 010667, p16 CH 011926, p17 CH 011887, p18t D 000374, p18b D 023450, p19 D 003623,
p20 CL 000122, p21t C 000381, p21b CL 000118, pp22-23 all images © Audrey Hale, p24t D 000851,
p24b CH 018567, p25 D 012564, p26, C001664, p27 C 003510, p28 C 003371, p29t D 004750,
p29b CH 018005

Contents

In the air   4

Call up   6

Battle of Britain   8

Shot down   10

On the ground   12

The WAAF   14

Plotting and tracking   16

Making aircraft   18

Air transport   20

Balloon defence   22

Ack-ack   24

Gathering information   26

Bomber Command   28

Glossary/Further information   30

Index   32

In the air

The Second World War (1939–45) was the deadliest war in history. Between 50 million and 70 million people died in total. Fighting took place on land, at sea — and in the air. Pilots, gunners, wireless operators and aircraft played a vital role.

During the 1930s, there was a world-wide economic depression. In Germany, an extreme right-wing party, the National Socialist (Nazi) Party came to power, headed by Adolf Hitler. Under his leadership, Germany built up its military strength, including a powerful air force, the Luftwaffe. In 1939, German forces invaded Poland. Britain, France and their empires declared war on Germany, which was later joined by Italy and Japan. The Second World War had begun.

> **"**Air fighting is a very detached sort of warfare being fought, as it were, between machines...**"**
>
> *Flight Lieutenant Frank Carey, 43 Squadron, RAF*

Tight formation

The Spitfire was a British one-seat fighter aircraft that became legendary during the Battle of Britain. Fighter pilots loved them because they were fast and easy to manoeuvre. They flew to battle in formation.

Air power

Aircraft had been used in the First World War (1914–18) and the Spanish Civil War (1936–39). But air power was even more important in the Second World War. Each side competed for control of the skies. Fighter pilots fought battles high in the sky. Bomber pilots carried out raids against military targets, ships (right) and ground forces. They bombed factories, railways and cities.

Information and support

Aircraft were used to gather information. Skilful pilots flew missions to take photographs for military purposes. Aircraft carried equipment and supplies, troops and parachute regiments. Military aircraft protected shipping and ground forces, and airlifted the wounded to safety.

A different world

Flying in 1939 was different from today. Aircraft were propeller driven and quite basic, but war forced change. More sophisticated fighter, bomber and transport aircraft were developed. Radar and aerial photography became part of war: so did area bombing.

> **"The appeal of flying is you are free from the earth. Your horizon is unlimited."**
>
> *Ernest Welding, German Heinkel 111 bomber pilot, Luftwaffe*

Circling

A British pilot circles an oil tanker in the English Channel, which is ablaze and sinking after being attacked by German bombers.

Call up

Men flocked to join the Royal Air Force (RAF). Recruits also arrived in Britain from other parts of the world, such as India and Canada. All were eager to take part in the fight against Nazi Germany.

Once war began, men aged between 18 and 41 could be called up for military service. Many volunteered. Flying was seen as romantic and exciting and the Royal Air Force was a popular choice. Some new recruits were already members of flying clubs. Others had no experience of flying. Most new recruits were in their late teens. Those who became officers had usually gone to private schools. Not all volunteers were accepted as pilots: some became gunners, ground crew or wireless operators.

Training

Trainee pilots were sent to an RAF training college and then to a squadron. Once war broke out, training was fast. Trainees learned with older instructors, some of whom had flown during the First World War. They flew fabric-covered biplanes (aeroplanes with two wings) and often took their first solo flight within three weeks. They learned how to take off, fly a

Distinctive clothing, 1940

Fighter pilots had no protective clothing and it was cold 9,000 metres (30,000 feet) above ground. This pilot wears his RAF uniform, leather flying helmet with goggles and warm flying boots. Many pilots wore inflatable life jackets.

straight course, spin, loop and land. They used compasses to navigate and if anything went wrong, were told to land in a convenient field.

Overcoming difficulties

Young men were also recruited from what were then the colonies and dominions of the British Empire: Australia, New Zealand, Canada, South Africa, India and the West Indies. Some overseas recruits overcame great difficulties to reach Britain. One 17-year-old Jamaican sold his bicycle and saxophone to raise the fare.

> **"**Most of us had never flown monoplanes before… suddenly we were faced with these fearsome… Spitfires. This bloke said to me, 'This is a Spitfire, get in it and fly it'…**"**
>
> *Pilot Thomas Neil, 249 Squadron, RAF*

Foreign pilots

Czech, Polish (shown here), Belgian and French pilots served with the RAF. Many escaped to Britain after Hitler's forces overran their countries. They wanted to continue the fight against the Nazis.

Battle of Britain

Vapour trails and darting aircraft filled the skies above southern England in the summer of 1940. British and German aircraft swooped and spun as they fought in the Battle of Britain — the first battle fought entirely in the air.

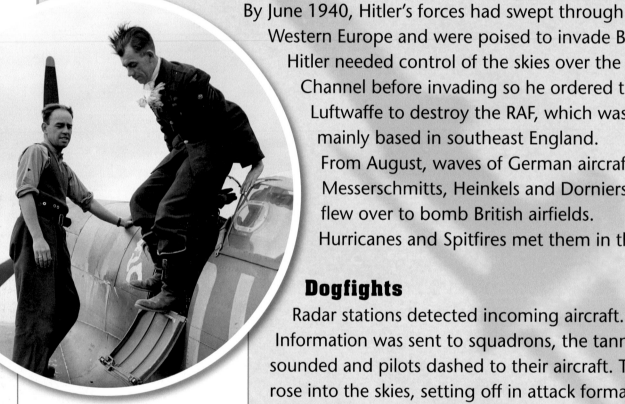

By June 1940, Hitler's forces had swept through Western Europe and were poised to invade Britain. Hitler needed control of the skies over the Channel before invading so he ordered the Luftwaffe to destroy the RAF, which was mainly based in southeast England.

From August, waves of German aircraft — Messerschmitts, Heinkels and Dorniers — flew over to bomb British airfields. Hurricanes and Spitfires met them in the air.

Dogfights

Radar stations detected incoming aircraft. Information was sent to squadrons, the tannoy sounded and pilots dashed to their aircraft. They rose into the skies, setting off in attack formation. Ground control barked instructions to the leader and battle began.

Battles in the air were called 'dogfights' and only lasted a few minutes. Pilots attacked head on, from behind, or dived down out of the sun for surprise. Spitfire pilots manoeuvred, kept a watch for enemy fighters, and fired their guns, using a firing button on their controls.

Grumpy

Flight Sergeant 'Grumpy' Unwin of 19 Squadron climbs out of his Spitfire after a sortie. Nicknamed 'Grumpy' after one of Snow White's seven dwarves, he shot down 14 enemy aircraft. Pilots who shot down more than five were known as 'aces'.

Scramble, 1940

When the tannoy sounded, pilots 'scrambled' to their aircraft. There was no time to lose. Sometimes pilots flew in their pyjamas. They checked oxygen supply, cockpit controls and soared off.

Opening fire

A German Heinkel bomber, photographed from an attacking Spitfire. When the machine guns opened fire, the noise in the cockpit was horrendous and the aircraft shook with the force.

Daily sorties

Young fighter pilots set off every day, sometimes several times a day. It was stressful and exhausting. Friends were killed but for many pilots it was an exciting time. The Luftwaffe outnumbered the British but failed to destroy the RAF. In September, the Luftwaffe switched to bombing British cities. And so the Blitz began, with nightly air raids that killed thousands over the next ten months.

Shot down

British civilians, particularly schoolchildren, watched the dogfights above them during the Battle of Britain. They saw aircraft exploding or falling out of the sky. Sometimes tiny dots of white appeared as pilots parachuted down.

Many pilots lost their lives in battle. Among RAF pilots, the death rate was 22 per cent during the Battle of Britain. Aircraft collided or were shot down. Bullets ripped through an aircraft's fuselage, injuring or killing pilots, and damaging the aeroplane. If a pilot could still fly, he attempted to get his damaged craft back to base, or he crash-landed. Some pilots parachuted to safety but often they suffered horrendous burns. The cockpit temperature in a burning aircraft could reach 3,000°C within seconds and pilots were often burned as they fought their way out.

Wreckage, 1940

This Messerschmitt BF-109 fighter crashed in a field near Hastings. The pilot managed to parachute to safety.

> "There was a big bang and my aircraft exploded. I... reached for the harness and slid the hood back. I rolled the aircraft onto its back... I popped out like the cork from a toy gun... my hands got a terrible burning... I [forced] myself to pull the metal ring of the ripcord... it took me about ten minutes to float down..."
>
> *Flying Officer Alan Geoffrey Page, 56 Squadron, RAF*

Parachuting out

Often petrol tanks exploded or caught fire when an aircraft was hit and pilots bailed out. Each pilot had a parachute, and within seconds of his aircraft being disabled, he had to pull the ripcord and launch out. Fortunate pilots reached the ground safely and many were back flying the next day. For the less fortunate, parachutes failed to open, or got caught in obstacles such as trees, killing the pilot. Occasionally pilots were fired on as they parachuted out.

Brave pilot

Sergeant G 'Sammy' Allard of 85 Squadron, RAF is congratulated on his return to Lille-Seclin in France on the evening of 10 May 1940, after shooting down the second of two Heinkel bombers claimed by him that day. Allard shot down 10 German aircraft in France between 10 and 23 May 1940. He added to his score during the Battle of Britain to reach a total of at least 23 by September 1940.

On the ground

The safety of fighter or bomber pilots depended on the hard work and dedication of their ground crew. Teams of mechanics, fitters and riggers often worked all night to keep aircraft in readiness.

Speedy workers

Spitfires carried 2,400 rounds of ammunition, 300 rounds in each of eight guns. Two armourers with two assistants could re-arm a Spitfire in about three minutes.

Members of a ground crew included fitters, who looked after the engine; riggers who took care of the airframe, and armourers, who were responsible for reloading the machine guns.

"… there was nothing worse than trying to change a tyre on a Spitfire. Without any modern tyre-changing equipment, it was RAF boots and brute force…"

Douglas Rattle, flight rigger, 19 Squadron, RAF

Ground crews worked at top speed to repair damaged aircraft that returned to base, and to re-arm and re-fuel them so pilots could take off quickly. It was like Formula One today, with ground crews stripping aircraft and carrying out repairs at top speed, but without modern equipment. When the call came to scramble, the crew started up the engines, checked petrol tanks — a Spitfire carried 386 litres (85 gallons) of petrol — and ensured that guns were primed and ready to fire.

Under attack

It could be as dangerous on the ground as in the air. When the Luftwaffe strafed airfields, ground crews leapt to safety as bullets rained down, shattering aircraft and huts. It could also be upsetting when injured craft limped back to base. Ambulances and firefighters rushed to the scene but ground crew often had to stand by helplessly as an aircraft crash-landed and burst into flames, with its pilot trapped inside.

From defence to offence

By October 1940, the Battle of Britain was over. RAF pilots continued to defend Britain against the Luftwaffe but also went onto the attack, with air raids on Germany. War spread out from Europe to Africa and Asia. Ground crew, like pilots, were sent all over the world.

> "… About seven or eight of us… watched a plane coming in. The pilot's flaps didn't work… he tipped up on his nose and overturned. We just stood there watching him burn to death. He was 19, 19!"
>
> *Fred Roberts, armourer, 19 Squadron, RAF*

Getting armed

Armourers prepare to shift two 1,000-lb (453.6-kg) bombs into the bomb bays of a Stirling bomber. Bombers carried huge bomb loads during raids on Germany.

The WAAF

During the war, thousands of women joined the WAAF — the Women's Auxiliary Air Force. They worked as cooks, mechanics, and in communications.

The Women's Auxiliary Air Force (WAAF) was first formed during the First World War. It re-formed in 1939 just before the Second World War started so that men could be released for combat.

Women aged 18 to 43 could join the WAAF, and many young women flocked to join. Some early recruits were from the wealthiest families but as war continued recruits came from all walks of life. They included hairdressers, clerks and shop workers. For most it was a chance to leave home, see the world and play their part in the war effort.

Instrument repairer

Leading Aircraftwoman Lilian Bader was one of the first WAAFs to be trained as an instrument repairer. A pilot's life could depend on his cockpit instruments working correctly.

Passing out, 1942

Standing on parade, newly trained and qualified WAAF recruits are inspected before being sent to their official duties. By 1945 there were 182,000 women in the WAAF.

" ... there I was, a small WAAF... in a heavy greatcoat, hat pulled down tight, carrying a gas mask, a tin hat, a case, a kitbag almost as big as me... clutching my orders and a packet of sandwiches...**"**

Elsie Bartlett, early recruit to the WAAF

> **"** We were all pretty young... only 19 or 20... we were laughing and joking... As we looked... one plane... was nose-diving to the ground... the mood changed. We realised it wasn't a great lark and... we were in for serious business... **"**
>
> *Jean Mills, WAAF plotter*

Balloons and spanners

Basic training lasted for about two weeks and then recruits were sent to their duties. At first WAAFs served as cooks, clerks and drivers. As war continued, and particularly during the Battle of Britain, duties expanded. WAAFs were mechanics, aircraft and radar plotters and interpreted reconnaissance photographs. They operated telephone exchanges, debriefed pilots after sorties, packed parachutes and staffed barrage balloons. They served in Britain and overseas.

Bravery

For many recruits, the chance to take part in the war was exciting. But the serious business of war soon took over. Hours were long and WAAFs came under fire during bombing raids on communications centres and airfields. They continued working despite difficult conditions and some were decorated for bravery. In 1940, WAAF Daphne Pearson rescued a pilot from a blazing aircraft, shielding him with her body when the aeroplane exploded. She survived and received the George Cross, the WAAF's first gallantry medal.

Flight mechanics

Wearing overalls, WAAF mechanics inspect a training aircraft. WAAFs did all essential work apart from flying and combat.

Plotting and tracking

The British public idealised fighter pilots. Less well known were teams of skilful men and women who took part in the air war, but from the ground. They tracked incoming enemy aircraft, guided pilots to their targets, and helped to bring them home.

Today, we take radar and long-distance electronic communication for granted but in 1939 they were still new. In the 1930s, a team of British scientists headed by Robert Watson Watt developed an early form of radar, known then as RDF (Radio Direction Finding). By the time war broke out, there was a chain of radar stations along the British coast. They sent out radio waves, which bounced off distant objects, sending back signals that warned of incoming bombers 160 kilometres (100 miles) away.

Passing on information

Radar screens looked like television sets, with wiggly lines running across them. RDF operators watched for V-shaped 'echoes', which indicated incoming aircraft. They telephoned information to filter offices, where personnel passed information through to plotters at central Fighter Command and operations rooms.

Bringing them home, 1944

A WAAF telephonist speaks directly to the pilot of a Lancaster bomber, helping to guide him home safely. She can hear his voice through her headphones.

Plotters marked information onto huge maps of England and, using map references, moved markers around to plot and track the progress of aircraft. Duty officers phoned through information to squadrons and pilots were scrambled. Ground control used radio telephones (R/T) to advise pilots about the positioning of enemy aircraft.

Tracking with tiddlywinks

Working in an operations room, WAAF plotters move markers around a map of England. The markers were little discs, like tiddlywinks. As information came in, plotters added markers so they could track the route of incoming aircraft.

Difficult work

Information flooded into operations rooms during heavy raids. Plotters and duty officers worked four-hour shifts around the clock. It was exhausting and everyone needed to stay alert to avoid mistakes. Personnel in operations rooms could hear the sounds of pilots' voices, which was sometimes distressing.

❝You didn't always know who was flying what unless you recognised their voices. It was a very anxious period, especially if they were shouting to each other, 'Look out, so-and-so on your tail, or so-and-so's gone down.' It could be very traumatic.**❞**

Edith Kup, WAAF plotter

Making aircraft

The demand for new aircraft soared during the war. British women entered factories to make them, and everyone saved 'Scrap for Spitfires'.

When war began, Britain had about 1,900 front line aircraft. Germany had more than 3,600. British factories produced fewer than 3,000 aircraft a year. The need for more aircraft, particularly after the Battle of Britain, was urgent.

Factory women

A Ministry of Aircraft Production was set up and factories moved onto 24-hour production, seven days a week. Some men were kept back from the forces as skilled workers but now women also trained as engineers. They learned to use lathes and precision tools, putting their new skills into producing aircraft. Women worked 60-hour weeks often for 11 hours a day. Some women also manufactured parachutes. They had to be carefully packed for fighter and bomber pilots.

Saucepans for Spitfires

British people were urged to save scrap for Spitfires. Aluminium pans and kettles were melted down for re-use. In fact, the aluminium was not suitable for Spitfires, even though civilians often wondered if their frying pans had been used for the Spitfire flying overhead.

Skilled workers

A woman works a machine in an aircraft factory. Women had to learn how to use complicated machinery to keep up with the demand for aircraft.

Dreadful conditions

Aircraft factories were often quite basic, more like huge workshops or machine shops. Some aircraft were produced in what one airman described as 'tatty old hangars'. Many women were horrified by their working conditions — damp floors, greasy walls, broken windows, and no hot water or separate women's lavatories. Factories were often bombed during the war, and air-raid sirens sent workers to shelters, disrupting work.

Increased production

Despite all the difficulties, new aircraft began to pour out of factories. In 1939, about 8,000 aircraft were made. In 1944, the number had grown to 25,600 a year. Aircraft design also developed. In 1939, the streamlined one-engine, one-seat Spitfire was the most modern British fighter aircraft. As war progressed different types were produced, including longer-range, two-engine, two-seater fighter-bombers, such as the Mosquito and the Beaufighter.

Tail wind

Aircraft worker Ruby May works on the tail component of a new aircraft. The wooden frame was bolted onto a steel frame, then covered with fabric and sprayed with acetate.

19

Air transport

Men and women of the Air Transport Auxiliary (ATA) ferried aircraft from factories to airfields. Aircraft were also used to carry troops, equipment and the wounded.

ATA pilots were civilians. They included men, who could not join the RAF for health or age reasons, and women.

Women pilots

Nearly 200 women flew for the ATA. They included British, American and Canadian women and women from New Zealand, South Africa, Poland, Holland and Chile. One famous pilot was Amy Johnson, first woman to fly solo from England to Australia. She died in 1941, when she crashed in the Thames. Some women were experienced pilots; others trained when they joined.

The first women

These three WAAF nursing orderlies were the first to be chosen for air ambulance duties (see next page). Despite dangers, young women were eager to volunteer.
Air ambulances evacuated some 10,000 wounded soldiers during the war.

Equal pay

The ATA flew aircraft from factories and workshops to airfields. Some were new aircraft; others had been damaged and repaired. At first women were not allowed to fly heavy aircraft, but soon they were flying every type of military aircraft. Pilots worked long hours and had to fly many different aircraft. Unusually for the times, women and men were paid the same.

'Flying Nightingales'

The RAF operated air ambulance services and nurses, nicknamed 'Flying Nightingales', flew with them to evacuate wounded soldiers after the Allied landings in 1944. As the aircraft also carried military supplies, they could not display the Red Cross and did come under fire.

> **"**One night I fell asleep in my Spitfire… when I woke up I was still flying straight and level…**"**
>
> *Marie Agazarian, pilot, ATA*

Ready to go, 1940

Dressed in full flying gear, women pilots of the ATA wait for their aircraft. Before the war, flying was a rich person's hobby. War brought in people of different social classes.

> **"**We were given a notebook… each page consisted of an aircraft and how to fly it… if we'd lost the notebooks, we couldn't fly the aeroplanes because every one was different…**"**
>
> *Jackie Moggridge, South African pilot, ATA*

Ferrying the wounded, 1944

Aircrew and WAAF nursing orderlies help to lift a wounded soldier into a Dakota in Normandy, France. Americans called them 'casevac' flights, short for casualty evacuations.

Balloon defence

Thousands of massive silvery balloons hovered over British cities, protecting them from low-flying bombers. The RAF thought women were not strong enough to 'fly' them, but they were wrong.

> **"**I volunteered to fly balloons... The doctor... said that we were mad and it was not a job for women as it was too hard and physical... [but] I was not discouraged... It was an exciting challenge...**"**
>
> *Audrey Heighton, WAAF, barrage balloon crew*

Corporal Heighton

Audrey Heighton, first from the left in the front row, was 21 when she started working on barrage balloons. She had to wear men's clothes at first — huge blue overalls tied with string. Later she got her uniform. She was made a corporal in 1941.

Filled with hydrogen gas, barrage balloons were attached to heavy steel cables anchored to the ground. Launching them and keeping them aloft was hard physical work. Operators called it 'flying' the balloons.

Repairs

At first, women were only used to repair damaged balloons. Women like Audrey Heighton, who had been a machinist before she joined the WAAF, sat at sewing machines stitching up tears. They also 'doped' or glued patches over the repairs. The smell of the glue and silvering on the balloon was dreadful and affected health. Women drank milk to counteract the effects.

Flying balloons

In 1941, with more men needed to fight, the RAF asked for WAAF volunteers to fly balloons. Audrey Heighton was one of the first to volunteer. She trained for 12 weeks before going to her first balloon site.

Women used a huge winch to launch balloons and bring them back to earth. They were not allowed to deflate balloons so they had to tie them down with sandbags and concrete blocks attached to the ropes. Women learned specialist knots for the work.

Teamwork was needed to keep balloons aloft. During high winds, women had to raise and lower balloons to prevent damage. It was dangerous as ropes thrashed about. One WAAF died when a rope caught her neck and pulled her into the air.

Women made excellent barrage balloon operatives, and there were many all-women barrage sites around the country.

Ack-ack

As enemy aircraft arrived over Britain, searchlights probed the skies, and the men and women of Anti-Aircraft Command tried to shoot them down.

Anti-Aircraft Command was part of the British Army but the RAF had operational command. There were anti-aircraft batteries along the coast, in London and all major cities, and in dockyards. Wherever German bombing raids were expected, anti-aircraft crews prepared to defend the country.

Defending airfields, 1941

A two-man crew staff an anti-aircraft gun to defend an airfield in Suffolk.

Complex operation

Hitting a moving target is not easy and most raids were at night. A dozen or more people staffed the big guns. Radar operators picked up incoming aircraft. Range finders worked out the range. They used a predictor to follow the aircraft's course, and a range finder device to work out where the aircraft would be when a shell was fired. Searchlight crews shone beams high into the sky to light up incoming aircraft and several people operated the guns — elevating them, loading shells and then firing.

Practice makes perfect

Anti-aircraft defence was skilful work. Training was important. Here, a WAAF projects targets onto a screen, and the gunner practises aiming his gun.

Ack-ack girls

At first only men staffed anti-aircraft guns, or ack-ack as they were known. From 1941, women were recruited. Many were still in their teens. They worked with men, sitting through long, cold nights wearing heavy boots, battle jackets, and hooded fur coats, known as 'teddy bear' coats. They did the same tasks as men, but were not allowed to fire the guns. Both men and women stayed at batteries, living in tents or huts if they were lucky.

> **"**A mobile bath unit was erected near one of the big anti-aircraft guns... the gun crew came across for a quick bath... they were... singing their heads off... the sirens went... eight cubicle doors flew open and these pink bodies shot out... leapt on the gun and started firing away...**"**
>
> *Marguerite Crowther, ambulance driver, London*

Guiding home

Germany used ack-ack as well, often hitting or disabling British bombers. As bombers limped back to base in Britain, searchlight crews shone beams to guide them back to base.

Guarding the Home Front, 1943

Members of the Home Guard manned anti-aircraft guns. Many had civilian daytime jobs and did anti-aircraft duties at night and at weekends.

Gathering information

From 1941, the RAF took a more offensive role against Germany. Longer-range bombers were developed and bombing raids intensified. Gathering information about targets was essential.

Taking photographs from the air was not new. During the First World War, pilots in biplanes had photographed the trenches but aerial reconnaissance — gathering information from the air — became more sophisticated and widely used during the Second World War.

The first development was to use fast, high-flying aircraft instead of bombers to take photographs. Spitfires were chosen for this role. Their radios and guns were removed, and cameras and extra fuel were put on board. Later, some aircraft were built specifically for reconnaissance.

Gathering information

Pilots flew speedy missions, swooping low over munitions dumps, airfields, shipping convoys, weapon sites, and other potential targets to gather information. They took photographs of sites, which were used to brief bombing crews so they could pinpoint their targets accurately. After a bombing mission,

Snapping planes

While on a reconnaissance flight to northern France, an RAF photographer snaps another aircraft in the sky — a Bristol Blenheim from 40 Squadron.

pilots returned to photograph the results. Flights usually took place during daylight and were very dangerous. Like the RAF, Luftwaffe pilots also flew reconnaissance missions.

Airborne missions

As well as carrying out bombing missions, RAF pilots took troops into war, in what were known as airborne missions. Pilots dropped parachute troops in Sicily, Normandy and in Germany at the end of the war. Bomber pilots towed gliders, which carried troops and equipment, then released the glider, whose army pilot flew it down to a specific target. Accuracy was essential. Crash-landings were common, and missions were often met by deadly enemy flak.

Damage
In April 1943 Bomber Command attacked a naval dockyard in Italy. As this photograph shows, they destroyed sheds, storehouses and workshops.

❝... my objective was a small corner of a particularly tiny field... If I overshot, I would crush us all against a 14-foot [4-metre] high embankment — if I undershot, I would destroy my seven tons of powerless aircraft and its human cargo... there was no room for error...**❞**

Roy Howard, Glider Pilot Regiment, Airborne Invasion, Normandy 1944

Bomber Command

From 1941, pilots and crews of Bomber Command carried out bombing raids on Germany. It was very dangerous work. Nearly 56,000 men lost their lives.

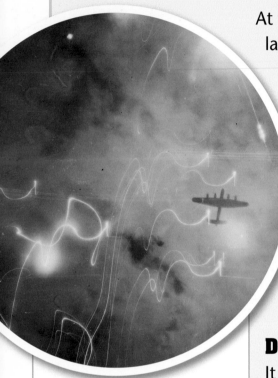

At first, bomber pilots flew daytime missions. Their large aircraft were easy targets for German fighter pilots. Bombing crews flew low, so many were unable to bale out.

Bomber Command switched to night bombing missions but there were problems. Navigation was basic. Pilots used compasses and estimated the position of targets by speed and flying time. Eventually, better bombers such as Lancasters were developed, and improved radar, navigation tools and aerial reconnaissance helped.

Night attack, 1943

Flares, smoke and explosions surround an RAF Avro Lancaster during a night attack on Hamburg, Germany. Radar was used for navigation.

Danger and discomfort

It was noisy and uncomfortable inside a bomber. It was also very cold, particularly for the rear gunner, in the tail of the aircraft. German anti-aircraft targeted bombers and shot them down. Laden with fuel and bombs, aircraft often exploded in mid air.

> **"** … there was a great bang… I felt blood running down my face… We were at about 19,000 feet [5,800 metres] down when — wham again… we started to spin down… I opened the bomb doors… kept her straight and level until I felt the bombs go off…**"**
>
> *Flight Lieutenant Bill Reid, 61 Squadron, RAF*

> **"During the Nuremberg raid… they were just going down like flies… it was a very hectic disastrous raid… dozens of planes going down and blowing up on the ground…"**
>
> *Flight Lieutenant Arnold Easton, 467 Squadron, RAF*

The most risky part was dropping the bombs. Pilots had to keep aircraft level and fly straight to hit the target. Even after bombs were dropped, they sometimes had to take photographs before flying home.

The end

From 1943, British and American bombers bombed Germany around the clock. Soon 1,000 missions were bombing dockyards, weapon sites and oil pipelines. Cities were also targeted such as Cologne, Nuremberg and Hamburg. In 1945, the Allies bombed Dresden, killing thousands of people. Even at the time, many British people were shocked.

In May 1945, Germany surrendered and the war in Europe was over. Thousands of airmen and women had died on both sides.

Survival rate

Following a night raid over Germany, a bomber crew is debriefed. Crews were exhausted after a mission. In 1943 only one in six crews survived one tour of duty, or thirty sorties.

Dam busters

In May 1943, 617 Squadron set out to bomb German dams in Germany's Ruhr district, using a new 'bouncing bomb'. They had to drop the bomb 18 metres (60 feet) above the water. They breached the dams but eight out of 19 bombers were lost in the attempt.

Glossary

Ack-ack Short for Anti-Aircraft.

Aerial Happening in the air.

Area bombing When many air raids target an area or a city, to destroy it.

Battery Four to eight anti-aircraft guns.

Blitz German bombing of British cities. It began in September 1940.

British Commonwealth Countries such as Canada and India, which were formerly part of the British Empire.

Dogfight Two or more aircraft fighting in the air.

Dornier (Do-17) German medium-range bomber, which carried a four- or five-man crew. Nicknamed 'flying pencil' because it was long and thin.

First World War (1914-18) Also called the 'Great War' or World War I. Fought between the Entente, which included Britain, France, Italy, Russia and the USA, and the Central Powers, which included Germany, Austria-Hungary and Turkey.

Flak Anti-aircraft fire.

Glider An aircraft without an engine that carried troops, tanks and other military equipment.

Heinkel (He-111) German bomber that carried a crew of five.

Home Guard A volunteer force of men trained to defend against invasion.

Hood The protective, see-through cover over the pilot's cockpit.

Hurricane British single-engine fighter aircraft, with a one-man crew. The Spitfire is always associated with the Battle of Britain, but Hurricanes shot down more aircraft.

Luftwaffe German word for their air force.

Messerschmitt (BF-109) German single-seat fighter aircraft.

Radar Stands for Radio Direction and Ranging, originally called RDF (Radio Direction Finding).

RAF Royal Air Force.

Reconnaissance Exploring an area to get information about enemy forces, weapon sites and ground conditions. Sometimes shortened to 'recce'.

Scramble RAF term used by pilots to describe taking off as quickly as possible.

Second World War (1939-45) Also known as World War II. Fought between the Axis Powers, which included Germany, Italy and Japan, and the Allies, which included Britain, Commonwealth countries, France, Russia and the USA.

Sortie Mission or attack flown by military aircraft.

Spitfire British single-engine fighter aircraft with a one-man crew. It was fast and turned easily.

Squadron A unit of between ten to 18 military aircraft.

Tannoy A type of public address system.

Tour (of duty) Thirty sorties or 200 flying hours.

Vapour trail White condensation trails left by aeroplanes.

WAAF Women's Auxiliary Air Force, the women's section of the RAF.

Books

My Second World War, Daniel James, Franklin Watts in association with the Imperial War Museum, 2008

War Machines: Aeroplanes, Simon Adams, Franklin Watts in association with the Imperial War Museum, 2007

Growing Up in World War Two, Catherine Burch, Franklin Watts, 2009

The Second World War, Dennis Hamley, Franklin Watts, 2007

Some useful websites

http://london.iwm.org.uk/upload/package/28/batbritsound/intro.htm
Imperial War Museum website where you can listen to pilots' accounts of taking part in the Battle of Britain.

http://london.iwm.org.uk/upload/package/27/battleofbritain/intro.htm
Imperial War Museum online exhibition about the Battle of Britain.

http://www.bbc.co.uk/ww2peopleswar/categories/c1183/
BBC website where you can read people's own stories of serving with the RAF during the Second World War.

http://www.bbc.co.uk/ww2peopleswar/categories/c1185/
BBC website where you can read what it was like to serve as a WAAF during the Second World War.

Note to parents and teachers:
Every effort has been made by the Publishers to ensure that the websites in this book are suitable for children, that they are of the highest educational value, and that they contain no inappropriate or offensive material. However, because of the nature of the Internet, it is impossible to guarantee that the contents of these sites will not be altered. We strongly advise that Internet access is supervised by a responsible adult.

Index

A

ack-ack 24, 25, 30
aircraft
   bomber 5, 9, 11, 13, 16, 18,
    19, 22, 25, 26, 27, 28, 29, 30
   fighter 4, 5, 6, 8, 9, 18, 19
   transport 5, 20-21
airfields 8, 13, 15, 20, 21, 24,
   26
airlifts 5, 20, 21
air raids 9, 13, 19, 22, 29, 30
ATA (Air Transport Auxiliary)
   20-21
ambulances, air 20, 21
Anti-Aircraft Command 24-25
Australia 7, 20

B

balloons, barrage 15, 22, 23
batteries, anti-aircraft 24, 25, 30
Battle of Britain 4, 8-9, 10, 13,
   15, 18, 30, 31
biplanes 6, 26
Blitz, the 9, 30
Bomber Command 27, 28-29
bombing, area 5, 30
Britain 4, 6, 7, 8, 9, 10, 11, 13,
   15, 16, 17, 18, 20, 22, 24, 25,
   29, 30

C

Canada 6, 7, 20, 30
communications 14, 15, 16-17
control, ground 8, 17
crash-landings 10-11, 13, 15,
   27
crews,
   anti-aircraft 24-25
   ground 6, 12-13

D

deaths 4, 9, 10-11, 13, 23, 28,
   29
dogfights 8, 9, 10, 30

F

factories, aircraft 18-19, 20, 21
Fighter Command 16
First World War 5, 6, 14, 26, 30
France 4, 7, 26, 30

G

Germany 4, 5, 6, 7, 8, 9, 10, 11,
   13, 18, 24, 25, 26, 27, 28, 29,
   30
gliders 27, 30
guns, anti-aircraft 11, 24, 25,
   28, 30

H

Hitler, Adolf 4, 7, 8
Home Guard 25, 30

J

Japan 4, 30
Johnson, Amy 20

L

Luftwaffe 4, 5, 8, 9, 13, 27, 30

M

mechanics 12, 14, 15

N

National Socialist (Nazi) Party
   4, 6
navigation 7, 14, 28
New Zealand 7, 20
nurses 20, 21

O

operations rooms 16-17
operators, radar/RDF 16, 24
operators, wireless 4, 6

P

parachutes 5, 10, 11, 15, 18, 27
photography, aerial 5, 15, 26-
   27, 28, 29
plotters, radar 15, 16-17
Poland 4, 7, 20

R

radar 5, 8, 15, 16-17, 28, 30
RDF (Radio Direction Finding)
   16, 30
raids, bombing (and see air
   raids) 5, 10, 11, 13, 15, 17,
   24, 26, 27, 28, 29
reconnaissance 5, 15, 26-27,
   28, 30
RAF (Royal Air Force) 4, 6, 7, 8,
   9, 10, 11, 12, 13, 20, 21, 22,
   23, 24, 26, 27, 28, 29, 30, 31

S

searchlights 24, 25
stations, radar 8, 16

T

training, pilot 6-7, 20

U

uniforms 6, 7, 21, 22, 25
United States 20, 21, 29, 30

V

volunteers 6, 14, 20, 23

W

Watt, Robert Watson 16
West Indies 7
women 14-15, 16, 17, 18, 19,
   20, 21, 22, 23, 24, 25, 29
WAAF (Women's Auxiliary Air
   Force) 14-15, 16, 17, 20, 21,
   22, 23, 24, 30, 31